Also by ... N. Doyd

The Love Book: Writing Your Way to Your Soul Mate

Gratitude Journal: 52 Writing Prompts to Celebrate Your Wonderful Life

The Science of Getting Rich Action Plan: Decoding Wallace D. Wattles's Bestselling Book

7 Days to Minimalistic Living: A Stress-Free Guide to Declutter, Clean and Organize Your Home and Your Life

Write Him Off

*Journal Prompts to Heal Your
Broken Heart in 30 Days*

Elizabeth N. Doyd

ISBN-13: 978-1987859010

ISBN-10: 1987859014

Contents

Introduction   7

PART ONE: Him   11
Day 1: Write It Raw   13
Day 2: Unfinished Business   15
Day 3: His Biggest Flaws   19
Day 4: Surrender   21
Day 5: Fears, Big or Small   23
Day 6: Safe Haven   25
Day 7: A History of Love   27
Day 8: All the Right Men   29
Day 9: Him? Or him?   31
Day 10: Bad Habits   33
Day 11: Ma & Pa   35
Day 12: Miss Co-Dependent   37
Day 13: Unavailability   39
Day 14: Beliefs About Love   41
Day 15: Forgiveness   43

PART TWO: You
Day 16: Dream Date   47
Day 17: The Blame Game   49
Day 18: The History Boys   51
Day 19: Your Worst Enemy   53
Day 20: Your Assets   55
Day 21: Love Those Who Love You   57
Day 22: Negative Cycle   59
Day 23: Biggest Hits   61

Day 24: Social Calendar   63
Day 25: Get Outside   65
Day 26: Top Ten   67
Day 27: Dinner Date   69
Day 28: Ideal Life   71
Day 29: Gratitude Journal   73
Day 30: Have Faith   75

Afterword   77

About the Author   81

Introduction

Every woman on earth has been heart broken at some point in life. Doctors and models, athletes and mothers—no one is exempt from this gut-wrenching experience. The cord snapped from a deep connection with a significant other can send you reeling into the dark unknown. No wonder you're scrambling to get things back to the way they were. But life is about moving forward, not dwelling on the past.

As vulnerable and helpless as you feel right now, there is something you can control.

Do you want to be the woman who lets one breakup, one measly man, shatter her world and keep her in perpetual pain and turmoil?

Or do you want to be the woman who walks out of this incompatible relationship with her head held high and straight onto the path of love and faith?

This woman is confident that she will be with the right man at the right time, and that this speed bump only has something to teach her along the way.

It may not seem like it now, but there is plenty to learn.

Writing is a great way of getting your pain on paper. Let yourself cry and indulge until you can't bear the sight of another piece of chocolate. Remember that emotion can be a funny thing. It has a cunning way of convincing you that it is real. It sustains itself through your belief that it is.

When emotions are down on the page, it's concrete. You can examine it with more rationality, and this gives you a better chance of releasing its hold over you.

Journaling can also help you uncover some inner blockages you may be unconscious of. By making the effort to write every day, you're taking the necessary steps to release your ex, but also your self-doubts and insecurities. As you write, you'll find that inner part of your soul emerging to give you the answers you didn't think you had.

Acknowledge that this will not be an easy time; expect the healing process to be uncomfortable. You opened your heart to someone, but you are not broken. Your heart may feel like it, but it's still pumping. You're still alive. If you didn't feel pain, you wouldn't be. You're braver than you think.

Give yourself the time to heal, and take care of yourself the best you can. Sometimes it may seem impossible that you'll ever get over him. You will. But it won't serve you to contact him. This journal will let you express yourself without the risk of judgment and without breaking your dignity.

You can do one journal prompt each day every day for 30 days, or you can pace them and take breaks in between if you find the work to be emotionally heavy. Either way, give yourself credit for making the effort to let go. Your journal is a safe place for your emotions.

A relationship consists of two people. The other person is always a reflection of us.

That's why this book is divided into two sections: 15 prompts that turn the spotlight on him, and 15 that focuses on you.

By taking responsibility in the role that you played in the relationship, you can let go of the toxic hold it has over you. You'll release some of the negative beliefs you may have about love, and about yourself, and then set a plan to build your self-esteem and faith in finding a more suitable partner.

It's hard to see a bright future when you're in mourning, feeling as if you've been sucked into a black hole. The relationship had once been a source of security and now the security is gone. But time really does heal. Track your progress in writing.

If you don't have a journal, buy one with a cover that appeals to you. Make sure it's comfortable to write in. Some people prefer spiral-ring notebooks so they can fold the pages. Use whatever works for you.

Have you ever kept a journal in your childhood or early teen years? When you read back the entries, don't they amuse you with their melodramatic urgency? In 30 days, it's entirely possible that you'll read back on your first few entries and shake your head with the wisdom of a woman who has lived to tell the tale and more.

When you've finished with the prompts, keep tracking your progress. Note the people, places, things and experiences you're grateful to have in your life. Write him off and write yourself into a life of love and joy.

— Elizabeth N. Doyd

PART ONE: Him

Write Him Off

DAY 1:
WRITE IT RAW

" *There is always some madness in love. But there is also always some reason in madness.*"

— Friedrich Nietzsche

Are you holding imagery conversations with your ex in your head? Ones where you get to say what you didn't get to say when your relationship ended?

Obsessing over what should have been is unhealthy and it sucks the positive energy out of you. It's exhausting to be fighting with him, even mentally, but the urge to communicate with him might be so strong that you want to pick up the phone (again) and speak your mind.

Do not contact him. He hurt you. Don't give him the chance to hurt you again.

Write down your feelings in your journal instead. What do you blame him for? What do you want to say to him? Are you angry with him? Do you miss him?

Use as many pages as you want. Pretend you're writing a letter directly to him. But do not send it. Do not contact him and read it out loud to him. Doing so will put yourself in great risk of being trapped in the same cycle of negativity.

This exercise should be a safe experience for you to explore your pain in order to put it behind you, not to stir up more arguments with your ex. If you're energized by this outpouring of emotion and feel a strong urge to share it, call a trusted friend instead.

DAY 2:
UNFINISHED BUSINESS

" *Sometimes the only way the good Lord can get into some hearts is to break them.*"

– Fulton J. Sheen

If you still have the urge to see him again in the name of closure, be honest with yourself. Is this just another excuse to see him? To make him realize that he was wrong? For him to see what he's missing and take you back?

Seeing him will postpone your recovery. Begging and groveling will not regain his interest. Don't bother dressing sexy and trying to bump into him either. There's a reason that he's not reaching out to you. Retain your dignity. A high value woman doesn't beg a man to love her.

Give him space and if he really loves you, he will come back to you on his own. Men often withdraw, unable to deal with their emotions. Let him be. Respect his distance.

This may be hard if you are constantly reminded of his existence on social media. If you have friends in common, don't feel guilty about pulling back from the group while you heal. If he lives in the same neighborhood, take a break from your regular hang-out spots for a while.

Make a list of everything you can do to remove his presence from your life. Some more examples: delete his contacts from your phone, delete his emails, block/delete him on Facebook and other social media sites.

If you work together, avoid his area of the office. Find a new bistro to eat at lunch for a while. If you have children together and can't avoid speaking to him, try to keep your discussion to practical topics, such as school pickup schedules. Define clear boundaries.

Yes, this process is extremely difficult. You've just ended one of the most intimate relationships of your life and doing all this gives it a tone of finality. Realize that he will be an addiction for a while.

Cutting him off cold turkey will be hard at first, but something you'll gradually get used to. If you can't do all the things on your list right away, that's okay, but the list is there for you to check off as you come to them. The sooner you do this the better. Pretend that he doesn't exist to you. You might not feel that way now, but you can fake it until you make it.

Write Him Off

DAY 3:
HIS BIGGEST FLAWS

" *I took a chance, I took a shot
And you may think I'm bullet-proof,
but I'm not.
You took a swing, I took it hard.
And down here from the ground I see who you are*"
— Taylor Swift

If you're stuck on all the great times you've had
with your ex, stop now. Harden yourself against
the fantasies.

**Recount all the negative experiences you've
had with him in your relationship.**

What are all the things that you can't stand about
him? **List all his flaws, big and small.**

Is he cheap? Is he lazy? A mama's boy? Inconsiderate with your feelings? Losing his hair? Getting fat? Was he hard to trust? Was he jealous and controlling? Did you argue too much? Did he insult you? Did he have bad breath? Did he flirt with other girls? Cheated on you? Never left the toilet seat down?

And what about his biggest flaw – the fact that he is not in love with you?

If you're still insistent on how wonderful he is, ask your friends. They'll be much more objective about him. The purpose of this exercise is to take him off the pedestal and to be aware of why he is not compatible with you. The relationship didn't work out for a reason. Or two. Or more.

Again, do not contact him. Record your thoughts and feelings on paper instead.

DAY 4:
SURRENDER

"*This is a good sign, having a broken heart. It means we have tried for something.*"

— Elizabeth Gilbert, *Eat, Pray, Love*

Okay, admit it. You still have fantasies that he'll change his mind, return to you, and you'll live happily ever after. As nice as that may sound, whether this happens is not within your control. Every person has free will and like it or not, his decision is something you must respect.

What you wanted is no longer possible. Needless to say, you're upset that he couldn't do what you expected of him.

Go ahead and write down all the frustrations you have about the situation in order to surrender to something that is beyond your control. Release all your hopes and dreams you had

about you and him as a couple on paper.

Remember that being in a loving relationship is still a beautiful dream to have. While he dropped out of the running, you will still get a chance to turn your dream into reality with someone else, someone who wants to be with you. Right now, it's okay to let yourself acknowledge the pain and anger that you have.

DAY 5:
FEARS, BIG OR SMALL

" *Love is an irresistible desire to be irresistibly desired.*"

— Robert Frost

Being in a relationship, no matter how flawed, gives you a sense of security. There's always a plus one to depend on for social events, a date for Saturday night, and someone to be there for you in a time of need. Who doesn't like the warmth of physical affection, the feeling of being safe in someone's arms? When you're single, the security blanket feels snatched from you, leaving you with a sense of fear and desperation.

Write down all the fears you are experiencing with being single.

Do you fear an unknown future? A broken home? Do you hate being the only single girl in your circle of friends? Are your family members pressuring you to get married?

There's always extra societal pressure on women to be coupled up, so much so that many women define themselves through their relationship status. It's only normal to have these fears. By acknowledging them and realizing why you have them, you'll be better equipped to move beyond the pressures and figure out what really makes you feel fulfilled. We'll get to that on another day.

DAY 6:
SAFE HAVEN

" *We waste time looking for the perfect lover, instead of creating the perfect love.*"

— Tom Robbins

It's important to feel comfortable and safe in your living space. If you once lived with him and now live alone, this might take some getting used to at first, but you can make your home into a haven by making it your own. Living alone can even be fun, not having to worry about someone else for a change. Relish in your freedom in having the place all to yourself.

Start by describing your room. How does it feel to be there?

Next, list all the ways you can turn your living space into a joyful place.

Do some heavy cleaning. Clear out anything that reminds you of him. Donate them to charity. Replace those things with new things of your own. For example, if you remove a photo of you as a couple, replace it with one of you happy with loving family members or having fun with friends. Buy candles, flowers, new furniture - anything to cheer up the place. Learn Feng Shui. Repaint the walls, replace the furniture. Change the bedding.

Your living space should only contain the things you love.

DAY 7:
A HISTORY OF LOVE

"*Was it hard?*" *I ask. "Letting go?"*
"*Not as hard as holding on to something that wasn't real.*"
— Lisa Schroeder

It's entirely natural to be missing your ex. He was an important person in your life and now he's gone, and this takes adjustment.

Write down what you miss about this relationship. What made you fall in love with him in the first place? What did he give you that you couldn't give yourself?

Getting over him doesn't mean you need to stop cherishing the good times you've had together. The space in your heart is boundless and you can afford to reserve a place for all the good experiences you shared.

Doing this exercise will help you see what worked for you in this particular relationship. It'll help you look for these positive traits in a future partner, or one that you can fulfill yourself.

For example, if you are someone who loves to hug your partner every day, it may not necessarily mean you want to hug *him* all the time; you may simply enjoy expressing love physically with someone you're close to. If you were taken with his dry sense of humor, you may also be attracted to other people with similar senses of humor. Maybe you have the same humor and you enjoy bantering with like-minded individuals. By isolating these positive traits, you will have a clearer idea of what you are genuinely looking for in a partner.

DAY 8:
ALL THE RIGHT MEN

" *Being deeply loved by someone gives you strength, while loving someone deeply gives you courage.*"

— Lao Tzu

List all the men who have let you down. Who are they? Were they important to your happiness, your self-esteem? Why do their opinions matter so much to you?

Doing so will help you understand your relationship with men—how you see them, and how you think they see you.

Remember, no matter how many men have hurt you, there are always good men in the world.

Now list all the men who have loved you and inspired you.

Can't think of anyone you know? Surely there are famous writers, actors, musicians who have enriched your life in some way.

DAY 9:
HIM? OR HIM?

"*Never allow someone to be your priority while allowing yourself to be their option.*"

— Mark Twain

Take a look at the list you wrote on Day 7 on all the things you miss about being with your ex.

What if there was another guy with all the same amazing qualities that your ex had, who would do all the same things with you? Maybe he's better in some ways. Better looking, more considerate, more fun.

If you were with this man right now, would you still be pining for your ex? Why or why not?

Write Him Off

DAY 10:
BAD HABITS

" *I was crying a little for the boy I had wanted him to be and the boy he hadn't turned out to be.*"
  – Gabrielle Zevin, *Memoirs of a Teenage Amnesiac*

By now, you're probably more conscious of what you think about when you think about him. Let's do some work to further eradicate the habit.

Write down the recurring thoughts you have about him.

Beside each thought, write a positive alternative. For example, if you are constantly thinking, "I was never good enough for him," turn that thought around to, "He wasn't good enough for me. I'm now attracting a great guy who appreciates me for me."

By being conscious of these thoughts and turning them around, you can train your brain to stop feeding you the same old slew of depressing, self-esteem crushing ideas.

It also helps to **plan in advance what you can do when the negative thoughts descend**. When it's too much for you, you can look at this list of things that take you into a better headspace. Do you enjoy watching uplifting movies or TV shows? Running outside? Reading a book? Visiting a museum? List them so you can lift your mood up when you need to.

DAY 11:
MA & PA

"*Listen to God with a broken heart. He is not only the doctor who mends it, but also the father who wipes away the tears.*"

— Criss Jami

Like it or not, our parents are our first role models when it comes to romantic relationships. Your subconscious has all these beliefs stored away based on how your parents behaved with each other and with you.

Explore the relationship of your parents. Are they happy? Do they fight a lot? Are they divorced? Did you grow up with a single parent?

Also observe your own relationship with each parent. What are some things you love about them and some things that drive you crazy? Do you resent either one of them for something?

When you're a child, your mind has little protection

from outside influences and you tend to accept what you see and hear as facts. For example, if your father didn't communicate with you enough as a child, you might have thought that it meant he didn't love you when he might have just been a taciturn man.

Unfortunately, we take these beliefs into our own adult relationships. You might find yourself in a situation where you are with a man with some of the same negative traits as your father. Some women attract the opposite of their father.

What are the similarities and differences between your father and your ex?

DAY 12:
MISS CO-DEPENDENT

" *It is better to be hated for what you are than to be loved for what you are not.*"
— André Gide

Being in a relationship has advantages, but many disadvantages as well. When you're busy being one-half of a couple, you might not have the time to do the things you love, or to even know what they are.

What did you do in order to please your ex when you were in a relationship? For example, did you go to football games when you have no interest in football? Wear certain clothes because he liked it? Cut your hair in a certain way? Worked your schedule around his?

Now is the time to get in tune with yourself, learn some new skills and expand personal growth.

Make a list of all the things you wanted to do but never got around to.

Do you love to read? Want to learn how to cook? Tap dance? Train for a marathon?

Next, develop an action plan to incorporate doing these activities into your schedule. Find out where you can take those Zumba classes and sign up. Commit to a running schedule for that marathon. Cut out pictures of the haircut you've always wanted. Shop for a wardrobe that pleases you. Now is the time to make yourself happy with no guilt. You deserve it.

DAY 13:
UNAVAILABILITY

"*Stuart needs 'space' and 'time', as if this were physics and not a human relationship.*"

— Kathryn Stockett, *The Help*

If your ex was distant or unavailable a lot in the relationship, what kept you around?

What were the advantages of loving someone who didn't love you?

This may be a good indication of how you feel about yourself. It could also be revealing of what you think is normal and expected based on how other people have treated you in the past (parents, former lovers, etc.), or from what you've observed in other people's relationships and marriages.

Write Him Off

DAY 14:
BELIEFS ABOUT LOVE

" *Of all forms of caution, caution in love is perhaps the most fatal to true happiness.*"
  – Bertrand Russell, *The Conquest of Happiness*

What are your beliefs about love?

Do you believe in the great love stories in movies and literature? Or do you think love is just a fantasy and real life is full of pain and heartbreak? Do you believe that no man can ever love you? Do you think that all men are cheaters? Do you think you need to look a certain way to attract someone?

How did your relationship fit in with these beliefs?

Write Him Off

DAY 15:
FORGIVENESS

" *D* on't cry when the sun is gone, because the tears won't let you see the stars."
— Violeta Parra

Can you forgive him for ending your relationship? Why or why not? If you can't, it's okay. Just be honest and write down how you really feel. When you read back on this in the future, you'll be proud of the progress you've made.

Write Him Off

PART TWO: You

Write Him Off

DAY 16:
DREAM DATE

" *You know you're in love when you can't fall asleep because reality is finally better than your dreams.*"

— Dr. Seuss

What is your idea of a perfect relationship?

Explore not just what you want from a partner, but how the both of you feel and behave in the relationship. Is there mutual trust and respect? Are you considerate of each other's feelings? Are you supportive of each other's careers and other goals? Do you have fun together? Play sports, sail, travel together? Be as detailed as possible.

Now take a realistic look at your relationship with your ex. Did he belong in your vision of an ideal relationship? Don't try to mold him into the guy you think he should be, but as he is.

Write Him Off

DAY 17:
THE BLAME GAME

" *If you judge people, you have no time
to love them.*"

— Mother Teresa

No matter how successful some women are in other areas of their lives, breaking up with a beloved partner can leave them feeling like a complete failure.

One person is never completely guilty while the other is completely the victim. It takes two to "fail" a relationship.

Whom are you blaming? Yourself? Him? Or both?

If you're blaming yourself, why? Do you feel as if you're not good enough to keep a relationship going? Is there something you should have done? Hold nothing back in your journal.

When you read the accusations back to yourself, do you feel they are all true? Why or why not?

If you're blaming him, can the things that you accuse him of be applied to you too? For example, if you are accusing him of being distant, are there any areas in your life where you are distant with him or with someone else?

A partner is like a mirror reflecting our best and our worst traits. At the very least, you can thank your ex for shedding light on the areas you need to work on. This way, we can evolve into more loving and accepting people.

DAY 18
THE HISTORY BOYS

" *All discarded lovers should be given a second chance, but with somebody else.*"
— Mae West

Think about all the guys you've dated or had relationships with in the past. What first attracted you to each of them? Recall their physical features, their jokes, their interests and personalities. Did you fall for them right away, or did attraction grow over time?

Now recall when you first experienced a problem in the relationship. How did you react? Did you break up with him, or did he?

It helps to make a columned list. If you had three boyfriends, list the positive and negative traits for each of them. **Compare the traits. Do you notice any similarities and differences? Do the results surprise you?**

Write Him Off

DAY 19:
YOUR WORST ENEMY

" *I* 'm selfish, impatient and a little insecure. I make mistakes, I am out of control and at times hard to handle. But if you can't handle me at my worst, then you sure as hell don't deserve me at my best."

— Marilyn Monroe

Did your ex make you feel bad about yourself in any way? If so, do you think his criticisms were valid?

If you feel that he did make some valid points, what was he right about? What can you improve about yourself so that you can be in a healthier relationship in the future?

Write Him Off

DAY 20:
YOUR ASSETS

" *We* accept the love we think we
deserve."

— Stephen Chbosky, *The Perks of Being a Wallflower*

Now that we got the negative stuff out of the way, show off your good qualities. Everybody has them.

Write down everything that you like about yourself.

Don't stop there. Ask your friends and family, the people who love you most. Ask them what they love about you most, what you're good at, your best features, and how you bring positivity into their lives.

There is no one else in the world like you. Now what makes you special? Be sure to read back on this entry, and add to it, especially on the days when you're feeling down.

DAY 21:

LOVE THOSE WHO LOVE YOU

> " *There* is nothing I would not do for those who are really my friends. I have no notion of loving people by halves, it is not my nature."

> — Jane Austen, *Northanger Abbey*

Who are all the people in your life who love you? Whether you have two close friends or ten, there are always people around to share your love with.

Studies have shown that friends contribute to your health and happiness more than spouses. If you don't have as many friends as you'd like, or have lost touch with them in favor of a relationship, reach out to them.

Do you have positive, caring, nonjudgmental friends? **If not, you're in need of new friends. Brainstorm all the ways you can meet them.** You can meet them anywhere—volunteer work, the gym, classes, the local coffee shop. Start doing some activities that you have interest in and meet like-minded people.

Just don't treat your friends as stand-ins for boy-friends, dropping them when you do have a date. Friendship is a two-way street. Respect and honor them as you would a friend onto you.

DAY 22:
NEGATIVE CYCLE

" *Darkness cannot drive out darkness: only light can do that. Hate cannot drive out hate: only love can do that.*"

— Martin Luther King, Jr.

Similar to the exercise from Day 10, **write down all the negative beliefs you have about yourself.** Do you think you have a fatal flaw that will repel other potential partners? Do you think you're too stupid, too short, too old, too fat?

Now turn that negative thought around. Every time you put yourself down, tell yourself the positive statement.

DAY 23
BIGGEST HITS

" *You've gotta dance like there's nobody watching,*
Love like you'll never be hurt,
Sing like there's nobody listening,
And live like it's heaven on earth."

— William W. Purkey

There's nothing better than music to lift your spirits. **What are some of the songs you can listen to whenever you feel sad about your breakup?** Try to avoid songs about heartbreak. Make a list of at least ten.

What are some of the songs you like to listen to in general to get your energy going? Make a playlist.

DAY 24:
SOCIAL CALENDAR

"*Sometimes it's a form of love just to talk to somebody that you have nothing in common with and still be fascinated by their presence.*"

— David Byrne

Too much alone time is dangerous. So is trying to distract yourself from your sorrows by overbooking your social calendar.

The goal is to have meaningful interactions with people. **Plan how you can balance out your schedule** so that you can honor your relationship with yourself and connect to the people you enjoy spending time with.

DAY 25:
GET OUTSIDE

"*Some women choose to follow men, and some women choose to follow their dreams. If you're wondering which way to go, remember that your career will never wake up and tell you that it doesn't love you anymore.*"

— Lady Gaga

You can only eat junk food and cry for so long. A bad diet and a lack of exercise is detrimental to your health. Take care of yourself. Just getting out of the house and taking a walk can do a lot for your vitality.

List all the ways you will take care of yourself. Make a commitment to start a fitness routine. Do you like yoga and meditation, or running and cardio? Signing up for classes can help because you're less likely to talk yourself out of going if you had already paid for classes in advance.

Make a plan to eat healthier. What can you buy at the grocery store or for lunch that will be beneficial for your health? Nix the processed food and the excess sugar. Buy fresh vegetables. Consult a nutritionist if you are not sure where to start. A healthy diet can do wonders for your mood swings.

Are you getting enough sleep? Try not to sleep too much or too little. Make a sleep schedule and set the alarm. If you're having trouble falling asleep, try listening to a hypnosis recording or using a phone app with relaxing sounds and melodies.

DAY 26:
TOP TEN

" *Once upon a time there was a boy who loved a girl, and her laughter was a question he wanted to spend his whole life answering.*"

– Nicole Krauss, *The History of Love*

This is a fun one. Using your past entries for inspiration, **create a list of the top ten traits you want in your ideal partner.** Maybe you have as many as thirty, but whittle them down to ten non-negotiables. They can be physical or non-physical traits. Rank them. Is it more important that he's loving or tall? Funny or brunette?

When you're finished, look it over. Does anything on your list surprise you?

DAY 27:
DINNER DATE

"*Happiness is not something ready made. It comes from your own actions.*"

— Dalai Lama

Tonight or tomorrow night, you're going to treat yourself to a nice meal. What is your favorite dish? And what will you have for dessert?

This is a great exercise to enjoy your own company. **Write the dinner menu for the evening. Make a grocery list of what you need to buy to make the meal, then make it...**Have fun knowing that you're putting all your love and care into feeding yourself.

Set up the table with candles and flowers. Put on some relaxing music. Enjoy every bite of your meal.

DAY 28:
IDEAL LIFE

"*So, I love you because the entire universe conspired to help me find you.*"
— Paulo Coelho, *The Alchemist*

Can you imagine yourself being happy without a partner? Why or why not?

When you love the other areas in your life, your life already feels full. When you don't, you might be looking for a boyfriend to fill the void.

Imagine that being in a romantic relationship is no option. **What will you do with your life that is meaningful, and brings happiness to you and to others?**

DAY 29
GRATITUDE JOURNAL

" *Love is patient, love is kind. It does not envy, it does not boast, it is not proud. It is not rude, it is not self-seeking, it is not easily angered, it keeps no record of wrongs. Love does not delight in evil but rejoices with the truth. It always protects, always trusts, always hopes, always perseveres.*"

— Corinthians 13:4-7

Make it a habit to write down three things you're grateful for in life. Even on the worst days, there is always something. They can be anything—a warm shower, a compliment from a stranger, your health, your family, good weather. Make it a daily practice to notice the little joys in life.

Come back to this list and leave room to add to it. Or you may be inspired to start a separate gratitude journal.

DAY 30:
HAVE FAITH

"*Happiness often sneaks through a door you didn't know you left open*"
— John Barrymore

Do you have small triumphs to share? Like that hour when you didn't think about him? Or when you spent time alone and actually enjoyed it? Or when you watched a happy couple walk by without feeling sorry for yourself? Take note of any progress you have made. They add up. They are proof that you are heading in the right direction.

Write Him Off

AFTERWORD

Praise yourself for doing the work from this book. Love is a feeling of fulfillment. Since your ex was not giving you that fulfillment anymore, it's only right to let him go. There's no need to rush to look for someone new to fill that void. By loving and honoring yourself first, you'll be generating your own love. When you radiate love and happiness, you'll attract the right person all the more quickly.

The funny thing is, once you're committed to this process, your ex might try to contact you. On an energetic level, he's probably sensing that he doesn't have a hold on you anymore. Stand firm. Reread your past entries and decide rationally whether he is someone you still want in your life. Don't buy into the things he says. Watch his actions. What if he goes back to his old ways? Are you really willing to go through the breakup process if the relationship doesn't work out again?

Remember that your ex, or any person, is not the source of your happiness. Love yourself first and those who love you will appear.

— Elizabeth N. Doyd

Write Him Off

Elizabeth N. Doyd

Write Him Off

About the Author

Elizabeth N. Doyd is the author of the bestselling books *Write Him Off: Journal Prompts to Heal Your Broken Heart in 30 Days*, and *Gratitude Journal: 52 Writing Prompts to Celebrate Your Wonderful Life*. She also works as a relationship expert and spiritual counselor, having studied Kabbalah, Buddhism, hypnotherapy, astrology and Reiki.

Originally from Montana, Elizabeth has traveled around the world and currently lives in The Hague, Netherlands, with her husband, son and two Scottish terriers. Her highly practical self-help books are for those looking for guidance and healing in love, wealth and self-worth, and how to live each day with love, joy and purpose.

Write Him Off

Elizabeth N. Doyd

Write Him Off

Made in the USA
Coppell, TX
02 December 2019